RISE
IGNITE THE PROPHETIC IN YOU

A PROPHET'S MANUAL

Toriana Brown

<hr>

Table of Contents

"THE PROPHETIC MINISTRY"

~~~~~~~~~~~~~~~~~~~~~~~~~~~~~~~~~~~~

~~~~~~~~~~~~~~~~~~~~~~~~~~~~~~~~~~~~

This teaching will be on the history of the Prophets to the functioning gifts, and what it entails NOW in the prophetic ministry.

Preface

If there is a ministry that has been grossly misunderstood and most refused, I must say that it is the prophetic ministry. I am not surprised about this; however. Religiosity and the traditions of man are always in the habit of fighting against anything that has the ability to do the greatest damage to its organization. Religion will try and discredit either the prophet or even cause other people not to understand the prophetic so that they can dissociate themselves from it. People often dissociate themselves from whatever they do not understand. While that is okay for the people of the world, it is not to be found true about Christians. Yasha (Jesus) said that it has been given to us to know the mysteries of the kingdom (Mark 4:11). Also, Proverbs 25:2 makes it clear that it is the glory of God to conceal a matter but the honor of kings to search it out. As kings and priests in Christ, it is our honor to search out any matter that seems to be shrouded in any form of mystery. We should be excited about searching things out because we have the wisdom of God and the permission of God to know anything we so desire to know (1Cor 1:30; Mk 4:11). This is why it is so important to understand the prophetic realm.

Introduction
Time of the Prophetic:

When did the prophetic begin? What is the time of the prophetic? What is the Prophetic? What is the Culture of the Prophetic? The answer to where the prophetic begins is that the prophetic beginning or origin cannot be traced to a calculated time in the earthly timetable. The reason for this is simple. The prophetic began in God and is God. God is the *I AM,* the Alpha and the omega, the *BEGINNING* and the *END* with no calculated time involved in his nature. **What is the Prophetic?** The words of God are simply prophetic. The prophetic is God's way of endowing men to access information beyond their natural realm and senses so they can give foretelling and forthtelling details. God has always used the prophetic to cause man to know and understand His ways. He has always used the prophetic to navigate the pathway of man into the glorious destiny He has prepared. The prophetic is an important spiritual and supernatural tool in the hands of God for the benefit of man. The **culture** associated with the prophetic is supernatural because you see and hear beyond the natural eye and ear. This culture of the prophetic should not be taken as mystical or beyond understanding. This is far from the truth. You should know and understand the prophetic. Not everyone will become a prophet but we all should be prophetic. One scripture that sums up the prophetic is Romans 8:14 which says, "For as many as led by the Spirit, they are the sons of God." **To be led by the Spirit is to be prophetic**. It is that simple. The Spirit is invisible and yet he leads us in the visible realm to see and hear what is in the invisible realm. How do you think He achieves that? The prophetic. You might say He (holy spirit) uses visions, trances, words from the scriptures, and so on. However, those are simply various operations in the prophetic and, it will be clearer as you read this book.

The bottom line is this: We must know and understand the prophetic. It is the will of God for you to do so. God has inspired me to write this book in line with that will. As you read on, the prophetic will be demystified and your understanding about the prophetic will be enlightened and broadened. I want to start with where the Prophets came to be about, and when prophets merged into society.

What can be traced is the prophetic office was seen manifested about 800 to 400 B.C. with the writing Prophets. However, the prophetic *gift* flowed outside of the office in the OT on many occasions, just to give you one account – *Enoch Prophesied – Scripture Jude 1:14–15 (Enoch was born 3384BC – left this earth 3019 BC)*

PART ONE: OLD TESTAMENT
PROPHET HISTORY

Background of the Prophetic OT: In the Old Testament, Prophets were called by God and filled with God's Spirit. Prophets spoke God's word to people who had in one way or another distanced themselves from God. God raised men and women to speak his heart to the rebellious people. Old Testament prophets were to speak forth the Will of God which He had communicated to the prophets by revelation. Although we see prophets and prophetess from genesis to the end of revelation, Prophets' writings appeared during the days of the fall of the Hebrew nation, also around the moments of the apostasy of the 10 tribes which was at the close of Solomon's reign, and Israel's 40-year golden age. That was when the writing ministry of the prophets began. The prophets gave a wake-up call as soon as people began to forget God. As it were, they were instruments in the hand of God to ensure that Israel never stayed out of God's will for too long. As soon as Israel started straying from the path of God, the spirits of the prophets would be stirred up by God to start speaking forth on His behalf.

Prophets, the spirit of prophecy, and the gifts of prophecy were all in the bible from the beginning of the prophetic reign. My focus here is to show you specifically the prophets in the bible. More so the **prophets** that wrote books, the timeframe within which they ministered, the kings they ministered under, and a little information on their personality and where they came from. Understanding the ministry of the writing prophets and their functions and how they operate can help you gauge your prophetic call/gift. Starting here I will show you about the Prophets and the books they wrote in the Old Testament:

- There are 16 books to 16 prophets (writing prophets) giving an account of the history of Israel

- There were about 63 Old and New Testament Prophets written in the bible, e.g., Elijah… 1 Kings 18:36 (853-841 B.C.), Manahen…Acts 13:1 (47 A.D.)

- There are about 83 Prophetic signs or expressions under the Spirit of Prophecy which includes the 70 elders of Israel (Number 11:25)

- There were 9 false prophets including Hananiah (Jeremiah 28:15-17)

- Major and Minor Prophets books chapters are not written in the time order in which they happened

- Minor Prophet books don't mean they were less important than Major Prophet books; it just means the books were shorter in pages

- The Writing Prophets lived in the 9th to 5th century and ministered in 3 separate time periods (see below)

Assyrian Period: Jonah-Joel-Amos-Hosea-Isaiah-Micah-Zephaniah-Nahum (8)

Babylonian Period: Jeremiah-Habakkuk-Ezekiel-Obadiah-Daniel (5)

Persian Period: Haggai-Zechariah-Malachi (3)

Here is the summary of the Writing Prophets, their history, the three distinct periods they were under, the kings, their personalities, and their ministry.

Assyrian Period Prophets

Assyria (Assihrya) was a nation in northern Mesopotamia that became a large empire during the period of the Israelite kings. The kings in the Assyrian period were Ahaziah, Jeroboam II, Jehoram, Jehu, Jehoahaz, Johoash, Jeroboam II, Zechariah, Shallum, Menahem, Pekahiah, Pekah Hoshea. Assyria connected with Palestine (around 855-625 B.C.) Their dark ways had a hold on Israel and Judah's kingdom nation. They came into full rule in 722 B.C. Prophecy was in order because of the spiritual direction that was needed for the Hebrew people in this period of time. This was also called the monarchical period. The monarchy was split into 2 kingdoms – 1. Jeroboam, Solomon's Captain, took the northern ten tribes, and 2. Rehoboam, Solomon's son, took the southern two tribes. The tribes are as follows:

Northern Tribes: Rueben, Issachar, Zebulun, Dan, Naphtali, Gad, Asher, Ephraim, Manassah, Levi. The Northern Kingdom had 19 kings in total.

Southern Tribes: Judah and Benjamin. The Southern Kingdom had 20 kings in total.

God's Prophets of the Assyrian Period: Jonah-Joel-Amos-Hosea-Isaiah-Micah-Zephaniah-Nahum (8)

These prophets came about in this Assyrian period, with all falling within the 700 B.C. period. The prophets focused on the spiritual decline of Israel and Judah in the Assyrian time. The emergence of the Assyrian empire caused disorder in Israel and Judah.

There was a need for Prophets to move forward to guide Israel and Judah, and to keep them from tumbling. Below is a summary of the prophets, their books, their reign, their assignment, and how God spoke His heart into the people through the prophets.

- **Jonah** "yonah" means dove. He was the son of Amittai. He ministered between 790-770 B.C. around 16 to 20 years. He was a minor prophet which simply means his book was short. He was a prophet during the second reign of Jeroboam around (782-753 B.C.). As a prophet, he anointed Jeru. He was a prophet after Elisha and before Amos and Hosea. Prophet Jonah was called to the people of Nineveh (capital of Assyria) to bring God's Judgement to Gentiles (non-Jews). Initially, Jonah fled his call. He fled to Tarshish because he was scared of the

Assyrians for, they were destroying the Jews. However, Jonah finally repented and obeyed his call in the guts of a fish. When Jonah reached Nineveh, he gave a warning that the city would perish in forty days *(Jonah 3:4-5)* and the people believed him, repented, and were spared. Jonah was a warning prophet. Jonah was the only minor prophet that Yasha (Jesus) Christ spoke of. He is also the only Old Testament figure that Yasha (Jesus) Himself compares to Himself. *(Matthew 12:39-41).*

- **Joel** "yo el" means Yaweh is God. He was the son of a man named **Pethuel** or **Bethuel.** He was a ninth-century prophet and a minor prophet. He ministered around 825 B.C. He was a prophet of the southern kingdom of Judah, a man of great spiritual wisdom, and had an acute gift of discernment. He was proficient in temple practices. Some say he was a priest. Joel is one of the shortest books in the Bible with 3 short chapters. Joel's name was mentioned only once in the New Testament in Peter's sermon *(Acts 2:1)*. Joel prophesied during the season of the plague of locusts *(Joel 1:4)*. He forewarned the people of Israel of what would come to the land in the days ahead. Joel eventually rallied the Israelites to fast and repent.

- **Amos** "amos" means burden. He ministered between 780-740 B.C. He was a native of the southern kingdom of Judah but a northern kingdom prophet, he was not part of Israel, but nevertheless was sent to Israel. He was not part of bands-sons of the prophets (school of prophets). Amos did not come from a family line of prophets nonetheless he was called into the office he was. He was guarding the sheep, tending to the cattle when God called him to Israel. Shortly after that, he began confronting Israel's neighboring countries for their meanness, but mostly Israel for breaking God's laws. He prophesied at Bethel which became the center of idol worship and the residence of King Jeroboam II, warning that the Israelites would be taken captive by the Assyrians.

- **Hosea** "hoshea" means deliverer or salvation. He was the son of Beeri. He ministered between 760-720 B.C. Many believe he was not just a prophet but a priest as well. He delivered messages to Israel because of their unfaithfulness and he illustrated this in his relationship with his unfaithful wife graphically showing God's love and faithfulness to Israel. He knew the nation's doom was inevitable so he prepared the people for impending punishment. Even though God looked hopefully to a time of restored relationship which is portrayed through Hosea's marriage, he nevertheless prepares them.

- **Isaiah** "yesha yahu" means Yaweh is salvation. He was the son of Amoz. He ministered between 745-695 B.C. Isaiah lived in Jerusalem at the time Judah was endangered by the Assyrians. He warned Jerusalem about idolatry and ungodly unions. He ministered about the deliverance of God's people in Jerusalem from the Assyrians. He warned about the enslavement of Jerusalem by the Babylonians. He communicated about the liberation of the Jews by Cyrus the Persians. Isaiah wrote more about the ministry of Yasha (Jesus) than any other Book in the Old Testament.

- **Micah** "mika yahu" means who is like Yaweh. He ministered between 740-700 B.C. Micah was a rural prophet from the town of *Moresheth*. Micah warned the people of the impending Assyrian and Babylonian forced entry and foretold the fall of Jerusalem and Samaria. The capital cities of northern and southern kingdoms. Micah was the first prophet to warn Judah about the ruins of Jerusalem and its temple *(Micah 3:12)*. Micah was the final prophet to the northern kingdom. Micah foretold the birthplace of the Messiah and the grandeur of the future kingdom *(Micah 5:2)*.

- **Zephaniah** "tzephani yah" means Yaweh is my treasure. He was the son of Cushi. He ministered between 639-608 B.C. Zephaniah ministered in a period when Judah went back to its evil ways under the leaders of Manasseh and Amon. He was a prophet during the period of young Josiah, the noble king. He banned Judah from worshipping the Assyrian and Canaanite gods. He foretold the destruction of pagan nations like Assyria, Philistia, Moab, Ammon, and Ethiopia. He foretold the destruction and restoration of Jerusalem.

- **Nahum** "nahum" means compassionate. He ministered between 630-610 B.C. They called him Nahum the Elkoshite. He was the second prophet that prophesied to Nineveh. Nineveh repented about 758 BC. However, it was not long-lasting. So, Nahum's mission was to declare destruction on Nineveh as a judgment on the Assyrians for their hostile actions upon other countries.

Babylonian Period Prophets

The Babylonian Empire was a nation that came to power around 625 B.C. after the ruin of Assyria and lasted around 87 or 91 years. The Babylonian period is referred to as the neo-Babylonian period. The Babylonians of this period are also referred to as Chaldeans. King Nabopolassar carried Babylonian dark ways into the westward, eventually replacing Assyrian power. Babylonian power continued to grow until 605 when Nebuchadnezzar established Babylon. King Nebuchadnezzar, was the king in Daniel's day. The Jews were enslaved by Babylon after the destruction of Jerusalem. The prophecy by Daniel was eventually fulfilled that Babylon would be enslaved by Persia and Medes under the leadership of Cyrus. The Babylonian Empire came to an end around (539- 536 B.C.). The kings were Josiah, Nabopolassar, Jehoahaz, Jehoiakim, Jehoiachin, Zedekiah, Nabukudurriusur II, (Nebuchadnezzar II), Belshazzarr, AmelMarduk, Neriglissar, LabašiMarduk, Nabonidus.

The exilic period was during this time and The Prophets in the Babylonian period are as follows:

Prophets of the Babylonian Period: Jeremiah-Habakkuk-Ezekiel-Obadiah-Daniel (5)

The Prophets of the Babylonian period dealt with chaos, confusion, and disorder. There is about a fifty-year gap between the prophets of the Assyrian period and the prophets in the Babylonian period. Here is a summary of the writings of prophets in Babylonian times.

- **Jeremiah** "yeremi yauw" means Yaweh will lift up or the lord exalts. He was the son of Hilkiah the priest and prophet. He ministered between 626-586 B.C. Jeremiah lived in a Benjaminite village close to Jerusalem named Anathoth *(Jeremiah 1:1)* where he also owned land *(Jeremiah 32:7-15)*. For most of his ministry, he was accompanied by Baruch the scribe, son of Neriah *(Jeremiah 32:12)*, and most of Jeremiah's ministry was focused on the invasion of Judah by Babylonian forces. Jeremiah was the most persecuted prophet. Jeremiah is known as the weeping prophet because he prophesied catastrophic events pretty much his whole ministry. He wrote lamentations and was a prophet in the period of the southern kingdom. Prophet Zephaniah and Prophetess Huldah ministered as prophets at the time of Jeremiah's ministry. One thing is for sure Jeremiah was a man full of love and compassion for Israel. He was a man people could trust...they knew if Jeremiah said he would do something he would keep his word. A man full of Integrity.

- **Habakkuk** "haba kuk" means embrace. He ministered between 606-586 B.C. He was the last of the minor prophets who ministered to the southern kingdom. He is the eighth of the Twelve Minor Prophets. Habakkuk functioned more like a priest than a prophet by asking God for mercy instead of declaring the message. Habakkuk's main prophecy was aimed at the kingdoms of Babylon, Persia, and Media. Habakkuk owned several estates which he had inherited in the land of Israel.

- **Ezekiel** "yehetzk'el" means God will strengthen. He ministered between 592-570 B.C. Ezekiel was consecrated as a prophet through a prophetic vision. Ezekiel was the final priestly prophet in the Old Testament. Ezekiel was an Edomite by birth, later converted to Judaism, and became a disciple of Elijah, he was raised to specifically rebuke his people. Ezekiel prophesied to the captives in Babylon using words, parables, visions, and many other symbolic acts. Ezekiel had 13 symbolic acts, one of them being Ezekiel's wife died and he had to remain tearless and mourn less at God's command. God called Ezekiel man of god. Ezekiel was not only a Nabi prophet but he was a seer as well. Nabi means to stir up in one spirit, to bubble up in one's spirit, a hearer, and to speak the heart and mind of God. Ezekiel is the 3rd longest book in the bible with 48 chapters.

- **Obadiah** "obadi yah" means servant of Yaweh or One who serves or worships Jehovah. He ministered between 586-583 B.C. This book is the *shortest* book in the OT with just 21 verses, Obadiah had but one matter and that was predicting the great fall of Edom.

- **Daniel** "Dani El" means My Judge is God, Daniel was of royal blood *Daniel 1:3.* He ministered between 606 - 534 B.C. Daniel was taken captive during Nebuchadnezzar's first attack on Jerusalem in 607 B.C. as a teenager. He faithfully served under 3 kings, Nebuchadnezzar, Belshazzar, and Darius. He received counsel from both Archangels Michael, *Dan 10:13* and Gabriel, *Dan 9:21.* He became a chief minister at the royal court in Babylon. God used him mightily through dreams and interpretation of visions. Daniel marks the third of four great periods of miracles in the bible: The time of Daniel and Ezekiel. Daniel saw a vision of the Messiah as the "Son of Man" coming with the clouds of heaven *Daniel 7:13-14.* Daniel had a specific diet (a consecrated diet) and a lot of Daniel's vision goes hand and hand with the Book of Revelations.

Persian Period Prophets

The Persian Empire's capital was Shushan. The Persian empire stood for 200 years. The empire included Africa, Asia, and Europe. The Persian Empire was founded by Cyrus in 536 B.C. after they overthrew the Babylonian Empire. This is considered the restoration period for the temples that were rebuilt. The first king of the Persian Empire was Cyrus, who delivered the decree for the Jews to return to their home to rebuild the Temple. Darius the third king, allowed the second temple of Zerubbabel to be completed. In the reign of Xerxes/Artaxerxes the 5th king, allowed the Jewish nation to be reformed by Ezra. Also, in this restoration period, Nehemiah led the rebuilding of the walls of Jerusalem. The Empire came to an end in 330 B.C.

Prophets of the Persian Period Haggai-Zechariah-Malachi (3)

The prophets Haggai and Zechariah encouraged the people to rebuild the temple. Both Judaism and Christianity survived in this time along with the Pentateuch. Some of the prophetic writings were completed in this Persian period. The Prophets in the Persian period are as follows.

- **Haggai** "haggay" means "festival of Jehovah. He ministered between 520-516 B.C. He is referred to as a "prophet" *Haggai 1:1; Ezra 5:1; 6:14.* Little else is known about Haggai or his family. Haggai was the first prophet in Jerusalem after the return from Babylonian captivity. The prophecy of Haggai is second only to that of Obadiah. He was a prophet in King Darius' term. Haggai's main focus was to build the temple so the worship of God could be re-established. Haggai's message to the people was to build the temple again because the drought and destruction were a result of the slothfulness of the people in the things of God. The people received the message and did as Haggai instructed. Not only did Haggai have this message, Zechariah did as well. The temple was built and finished in 516 B.C., (*Ezra 6:15*). Haggai proved to be one of the most successful prophets at that time. Haggai taught on faithfulness, and his teachings were very effective and successful in the rebuilding of God's kingdom.

- **Zechariah** "zekari yah" means Yahweh is my remembrance. He was the son of Berechiah and the grandson of *Iddo*. He ministered between 520-516 B.C. Iddo was one of the priests who returned to Jerusalem in the group led by Zerubbabel (*Neh. 12:4, 16; Ezra 5:1; 6:14*). Zechariah was "murdered between the temple and the altar (*Matthew 23:35 and Luke 11:51*). Zechariah, along with Haggai prophesied to the returned Jewish exiles between 520 and 518 B.C. He helped build the temple 520-516 B.C. Jewish tradition states that Haggai, Zechariah, and Malachi were the founders of the **Great Synagogue**. He had 8 visions in one night *Zech 1-6*. God revealed to Zechariah that no matter what it looked like Elohim was in control of history and that blessings were coming to the faithful. Zechariah and Isaiah spoke more about Yasha/Savior than any other prophets. Including His death *Zech 12:10*. Zechariah is the longest book of the twelve minor prophets.

- **Malachi** "malachi" means my messenger. He ministered between 450-400 B.C. He was a fifth-century B.C. prophet. Malachi's main focus was to restore Israel to God. He did this by prophesying about the priests' financial abuses & neglect of tithes *Mal. 3:5-10.* He spoke of repentance from intermarriage with pagans & divorcing their wives to marry pagan women, not honoring their covenants and their relationships, both with God and with each other, which were failing. *Mal. 2:10-16.* Malachi emphasized the coming of John the Baptist who is to forerun the coming of the Lord. The book of Malachi closes the Old Testament and a prophet is not revealed in the Scriptures for approximately 400 years until the beginning of the New Testament.

As you can see 16 prophets wrote 16 books. However, there were many more prophets and prophetesses in the Old Testament e.g., Elisha, Elijah, Huldah, and Deborah. A closer study of their lives will uncover what type of gifts they had, how they operated, what type of kingship they were under, and why God had them help the house of Israel. One thing is this: there is not much difference between the way the Old Testament prophets operated and how we operate today. The only difference is we live under the Grace of Yasha (Jesus). God still communes with us and gives us instruction for the nations, people, events, etc. We still operate in all functions e.g., healing, and deliverance just like Elijah, Deborah, and more of the Old Testament PROPHETS. The style of the Prophetic Ministry is still the same. You just have to know what level God is instructing you to serve in. Showing the periods and the prophets in the Old Testament will give you an idea of how you may function in your gift and how God can use you. I know for me my call was after Ezekiel 3:1-11. As for me, God specifically wanted my life to be a scroll so when I minister to his people, they can see God's word in the words I speak with the style he has given me along with accepting the call.

Next, we will go into prophets in the New Testament. As we move forward, it will help you understand prophecy, the gift and spirit of prophecy along with the office so you can understand what level you operate in or will operate in.

PART TWO: NEW TESTAMENT PROPHETS TODAY

New Testament Prophets

The Prophetic Ministry has so many facets to it. One can operate and experience God in so many ways. We know that Visions, Dreams, Angelic Visitations, Spiritual Trances, Transport, and more happened to Daniel. *Daniel 1:17*, Ezekiel *Ezekiel 1:1*, Joseph *Matt 1:20*, Mary *Luke 1:26-28*, Peter *Acts 10:10*, John *Revelation 1:9-20*, Paul *2 Corinthians 12:2* and so many more in the bible. Most Seers experience these facets but anyone in the prophetic ministry can have these operate in their life as well. For one I am a byproduct of a trance as it is how I came to know my calling as a Prophet today. There have been many in the end-time remnant church that experienced the same facets of the prophetic ministry and will experience this more and more as the New Testament church is released in its full operation. Get ready church, it is going to be dynamic.

Background of the Prophetic in the New Testament church

The Prophetic Office remained relevant right into the New Testament times from the Old Testament. There are New Testament prophets, e.g., Yasha (Jesus) was a Prophet, Anna, Manean, and more. It is still valid and useful for the church today. The Prophetic Ministry is alive and well in the New Testament church today. In the bible, there were about 63 prophets, 19 of whom were in the New Testament including the 2 witnesses in Revelation. (this does not include any of the apostles). The word "prophet" is written about 140 times in the New Testament and over 300 times in the Old Testament. Female Prophet "prophetess" is used in the New Testament 2 times and in the Old Testament 6 times. There is much to be said about this matter in the New Testament church. Before we delve into the Office of Prophet, I want to go over Prophecy which is a big part of the Prophetic Ministry in the Bible and today.

- **Greek:** prophēteuō - prophesy- a verb means to foretell events, to speak under the inspiration of God...*Strong Concordance #4395*

- **Greek:** propheteia - prophecy – a noun means prediction in nature, bringing forth the heart and mind of God...prophecy is typically through his prophets *Strong Concordance #4394*

- **The** word prophecy was written 17 times in the New Testament

Prophecy is the direct link to God where we commune with him, dialoguing back and forth to deliver ultimately what he wants done on this earth. Prophecy brings forth that relationship with God to his people to encourage them and ultimately bring them closer to him. In today's world, prophecy has to line up with the word of God (bible) and always uplift the triune – The Father, Yasha (Jesus), and the Holy Spirit. Even though we are talking about prophecy, Paul speaks on prophesy being the desired gift *1 Corinthians 14:1.*

Today when we release prophecy, people can judge the prophecy in several ways:

1. Prophecy has to line up with the written word (Bible)!

2. Prophecy…the word you deliver to someone, does it bring the fruit of freedom or bondage?

3. Prophecy has to bring you back to **Yasha (Jesus)**!

4. Prophecy edifies, exhorts, and comforts!

New Testament prophecy has three elements to the prophetic realm. These elements are based around the Prophetic Ministry and are still being used today to get God's heart and mind across to his people. The Three elements of this realm are The Spirit of Prophecy, The Gift of Prophecy, and The Office of the Prophet. Let's look at these Three elements of prophecy a little closer. First the Spirit of Prophecy.

I truly love the operation of the Spirit of Prophecy because you don't have to walk in the vocation or the ascension gift of a prophet to be used by God to speak a word. The spirit of prophecy can operate anywhere the Holy Spirit sees fit to use anyone.

First Element
Spirit of Prophecy

Spirit of Prophecy is in operation when an inspired word or vision is released by the Holy Spirit into a person's heart to bring forth a word to God's people. Remember, it should always bring you back to Yasha (Jesus) Rev *19:10*. The Spirit of Prophecy can function at different times and different places for instance:

- It can function when a person is around a band of prophets or someone who operates in the gift of prophecy

- It can function in church or ministry events after or during an intense and intimate session of worship

- It can also operate anywhere there is a group of believers, e.g., prison, hospital, nursing home

- Or in your private time with God

This is where a strong presence of the Lord is in the atmosphere and it becomes easy for the spirit of prophesy to move!

Biblical Examples:

- Simeon sees God's Salvation *Luke 2:25-26*

- Zacharias Prophecy *Luke 1:67-69*

- The seventy elders of Israel *Numbers* 11:25 *O.T.*

Second Element
The Gift of Prophecy (<u>1 Cor 12:10</u>)

This gift is by the Holy Spirit as a body ministry function; it is without repentance. You don't have to be prayed up to operate in this gift as it is a piece of your DNA. This is where you just know things; it comes naturally out of you. You can look at someone, see a picture, or be in a conversation and this gift just pops up. Anyone in the body of Christ can receive the gift of prophecy and can prophesy; it is the most desired gift Paul talks about in *1 Corinthians 14:1-4*. With the Gift of Prophecy, you operate by grace and faith *Rom 12:6*. This is the second element of prophetic ministry. There are two purposes for the gift of prophecy and they are:

- **Forth-telling**: pertains to the present situation, declaring a clear word to someone. Edification, exhortation, and comfort typically come from this purpose.

- **Foretelling:** foresees the future by declaring the will of God for his people in a specific and direct way. *Prophesy* typically comes from foretelling.

The gift of prophecy's main functions :

- **Edification:** exhortation and comfort to the Body of Christ *1 Corinthians 14:3.*

- **Revelation**: Greek *apokalypsis* (noun), the revealing of someone or an event that was hidden, to bring to light *1 Corinthian 2:10, Strong Concordance #602*

- **Interpretation**: Greek *diermēneuō (verb)* to unfold the meaning of what is said, seen, explain, or expound *Daniel 2:16, Strong Concordance #1329*

As you can see the gift of prophecy has several major ingredients to it. Along with edifying, exhorting, and comforting, it is imperative that when you speak forth what God is saying you just don't give the revelation but the interpretation as well. It will be considered an injustice to do one without the other because a revelation of something can be literal or symbolic and one must speak the correct word of what is revealed and the only way that can be done is to take the time for the interpretation. The more you do this; the interpretation comes to you quickly.

The Third Element
Office of the Prophet

Prophecy in the office of the prophet is only 10% of the call. Prophecy is a byproduct of the office but not the main call. Even though it is only 10% of the office it is a vital element to help the Prophet deliver God's heart to the people. The Prophet uses the prophecy to help the church come out of complacency and grow into the kingdom it is called to be.

Now that we have gone over the Three elements of Prophecy. I want to help you understand The office of the Prophet (an ascension gift-Ephesian 4:7-11). Well, go over different types of prophets and some of the key components of a Prophet's Call. As you seek God more in your office this section will help you recognize what type of Prophet God has called you to be.

Office of the Prophet:

Prophets are called by God from the womb, some say a man can make you a prophet, however, it appears God creates the prophet at the first sign of the heartbeat in the womb. Before anything is formed you are his prophet. The prophet's office can only be affirmed by man. They simply just confirm what God has already stamped or bring forth what God has already stamped.

The main functions of the office of the prophet are to warn, break, uproot, rebuke, expose, give correction, activate spiritual gifts, build, train, equip, cultivate people's destiny, affirm, establish, teach, ordain leaders and so much more.

Other key roles of a prophet are:

- Interpreting Dreams, watch, judge, guard, protect

- Corrects spiritual climates, unlocking times and seasons, tearing down, planting, water

- Intercession that includes weeping, mourning, moans, laments

- Corrects religiosity, tradition, and carnality in men, break, open things, close things, plow, restore, counsel

- Worshippers

- Calls people to repentance, deliver, heal, bind, loose, repair, comfort, and bring change of business.

There are different types of prophets:

- **Nabi** means to bubble up, the word of God in you rises to the surface of your spirit. Nabi is the most common word used for prophet. *Nabi,* or a prophet, is a spokesperson, one who transfers the will and plans of God in the atmosphere, declaring the messages of God.

- **Roeh** means to see. To recognize and identify, unveil what is hidden from the natural eye to uncover secrets. Roehs have visions and dreams. A roeh can be described as one who sees pictures or envisions.

- **Chozeh** means an advanced extension of the roeh prophet. They are counselors, advisors, and walks in wisdom. They have commercial or cartoon-like full-blown visions and or spiritual trances shown right in front of them.

- **Marketplace Prophet** means one who functions mainly in a secular environment like their job. Pretty much one who is a prophet outside of the church and operates in some form of business.

- **Nataph** means to prophesy, to preach. Nataphs receive droplets of revelations from heaven.

- **Evangelistic Prophet** means a prophet that is not settled in one church but travels all over the world bringing the Gospel of Yasha (Jesus) to the lost, advancing the kingdom of God with the prophetic edge and supernatural ministry like miracles signs and wonders.

- **Shamar** means to guard, watch, observe, and protect. They learn the structure and conspiracy of the enemy from the face of God so they can thwart the enemies' plans using the strategic details God gives them.

- **National Prophet** declares the will of God to nations and the world government. Such prophets can see into territories that the enemy has struck as his own and bring correction to climates, to the body called Church, and also to the whole world for God.

Another key component of a Prophet's life is to function in the **9 gifts of the spirit** (*1 Corinthians 12:1-11*). I like to break them up into 3 sections!

Eye-opening/Revelatory Gifts:

Word of Knowledge – supernatural knowledge to reveal a plan and or a thing that you would not normally know in your natural state of the present and past.

Word of Wisdom - supernatural awareness of the future and to see into problems, situations, and purpose.

Discerning of Spirits – supernaturally brings to light what spirit is operating in a person or the atmosphere. This gift can discern the Holy Spirit, Demonic Spirit, Angels, or Human Nature Soul.

Power Gifts:

Gift of Faith - supernatural power gift of faith is to help us to believe the unseen and the impossible.

Working of Miracles - supernatural power gift to move in the natural and stabilize a natural formula that has gone wrong.

Gifts of Healing - supernatural power gift to heal without the aid of a doctor or medicine.

Declaration/Utterance Gifts:

Gift of Prophecy – supernatural divine word to edify, exhort, and comfort.

Diverse kinds of Tongues – supernatural languages unknown to the utterer.

Interpretation of tongues - supernatural gift to translate the unknown language.

In the earlier portion of this book, we talked about various aspects of writing prophets, history, the gift of prophecy, the prophetic ministry, and prophets in both The Old and New Testaments. The question now is what do you do to ignite the Prophetic in You?

How to Ignite the Prophetic In You

Activation. Thats right! Now it is time to ignite the prophetic in you through activation. We are going to be discussing how to activate the Prophetic in you. In order to do that, we are going to explore different tones of the prophetic gift. For this manual to bless you maximally, I want you to be open-hearted. Be ready to learn and step into this arena. Do not be afraid. For many, fear is the main obstacle stopping them from prophesying either in private or in public. For sure, the Spirit of God is inspiring them but some are too fearful to speak forth the prophecy in them. However, upon activating the prophetic in you. Confidence and boldness will be your portion as you walk in the prophetic. Ok Ready? Read on.

Introduction

In our discussion of the New Testament Portion of this book, I explained the three elements of Prophecy. In it, I distinguished between the Spirit of Prophecy, The Gift of Prophecy, and the Office of a Prophet. Let's reiterate!

The Spirit of Prophecy is in operation when an inspired word or vision is released by the Holy Spirit into a person's heart to bring forth a word to God's people. It is a manifestation of the Holy Spirit (1 Corinthians 12:10) and any believer can walk in it. The Gift of Prophecy is by the Holy Spirit as a body ministry function; it is without repentance. You don't have to be prayed up to operate in this gift as it is a piece of your DNA. This is where you just know things; it comes naturally out of you. ***"Having then gifts differing according to the grace that is given to us, let us use them: if prophecy, let us prophesy in proportion to our faith"*** (Romans 12:6)

Then, there is the office of the Prophet. This refers to an individual called to the office of a Prophet. The office of a prophet is a ministry gift or ascension gift of Christ. That is what is referred to in

Ephesians 4:11, *"And He Himself gave some to be apostles, some prophets, some evangelists, and some pastors and teachers."* The same is referred to in 1 Corinthians 12:28 *"And God has appointed these in the church: first apostles, second prophets, third teachers…"*

Having these explanations in mind, **how exactly do you ignite the prophetic in you?** Igniting is that supernatural flow that comes out from within you by the Holy Spirit. **Hearing God's Voice and Speaking in tongues is a big part of that…**

Prophesy is a big part of that... Hearing God's voice is a way all can prophesy. Speaking in tongues is a doorway into the Prophetic along with all the supernatural gifts of the Spirit. **"He who speaks in a tongue edifies himself, but he who prophesies edifies the church. I wish you all spoke with tongues, but even more that you prophesied; for he who prophesies is greater than he who speaks with tongues, unless indeed he interprets, that the church may receive edification *1Corinthians 14:4-5*.** Although you can prophesy from speaking with tongues, as you mature in the gift of prophecy the goal is to be able to hear without speaking in tongues." Once the holy spirit ignites prophecy in you, a plethora of the prophetic can and will flow out of you.

There are some simple truths that you should understand to ignite the Prophetic in you.

- **Be Born Again.** Let me not assume that you are born again. The first thing is you have to make sure you belong to the family of God. Salvation is a gift that is made available to those who repent, believe, and confess that Yasha (Jesus) is Lord and that He died and rose from the dead to save mankind (Acts 16:31; Romans 10:9-10). This gift cannot be earned through good deeds or by simply being "good" (Ephesians 2:8; 1 Timothy 1:9). It is a matter of faith (acting out on what you believe according to God's Word concerning salvation). You do that by receiving Yasha (Jesus), as your Lord and personal Savior. If you want to receive Yasha (Jesus), why not pray this prayer in faith: **"Heavenly Father, I come to You in the Name of Yasha (Jesus), Your Word says, "Whosoever shall call on the name of the Lord shall be saved" (Acts 2:21). I am calling on You. I pray and ask Yasha (Jesus), to come into my heart and be Lord over my life according to Romans 10:9-10. "If thou shalt confess with thy mouth the Lord Jesus, and shalt believe in thine heart that God hath raised him from the dead, thou shalt be saved." I do that now. I confess that Yasha (Jesus), is Lord, and I believe in my heart that God raised Him from the dead."** If you have just prayed that, you are born again. Halleluiah! Glory!

- **Be filled with the Spirit**. If you have not been baptized in the Spirit, this is the time to do so. The Lord Yasha (Jesus) promised us the Spirit.

"Nevertheless, I tell you the truth. It is to your advantage that I go away; for if I do not go away, the Helper will not come to you; but if I depart, I will send Him to you." (John 16:7.) He also said if you ask the Father, you will be filled with the Spirit. *"If you then, being evil, know how to give good gifts to your children, how much more will your heavenly Father give the Holy Spirit to those who ask Him!"* (Luke 11:13).

So, if you are not yet filled with the Spirit, why not ask the Father? Once you ask God in faith, he fills you with his Spirit. You can pray this, *Father, I thank you for the gift of the Holy Spirit. I recognize my need for your power to live in this world. I ask you Father to baptize me with the holy spirit right now as you did the disciples on the day of Pentecost (Acts 2:1-5). Holy Spirit you are welcome in my life. By faith, I receive your spirit right now. Thank you, Lord, I lift my hands and heart up to you right now in Yasha Mighty Name I Pray Amen.* "Now, just open your mouth and let new tongues flow as the Spirit of God gives you utterance. (Acts 2:4)

- **Desire to Prophesy**. Begin to build the desire to prophesy. Anticipate it. Paul said, *"desire spiritual gifts, but especially that you may prophesy."* (1 Corinthians 14:1).

- **Have a Proper mindset**. Paul taught the mindset to have regarding the manifestations of the Spirit. He said, *"Even so you since you are zealous for spiritual gifts, let it be for the edification of the church that you seek to excel."* (1 Corinthians 14:12)

- **Stir up the gift of God in you.** Use your gift. This is a way to stir it up. Paul admonished the young Pastor, Timothy to stir up his gift in 2 Timothy 1:6 *"Therefore I remind you to stir up the gift of God which is in you through the laying on of my hands."* Another way to stir up the gift is by speaking in other tongues. Begin to take time to speak in other tongues. This is a secret weapon of the Holy Spirit. It strengthens you. It helps develop the gift that is within you. Apostle Paul. He wrote to the Corinthian Church, *"I thank my God I speak with tongues more than you all"* (1 Corinthians 14:18). When you speak in tongues, you not only ignite the prophetic in you. You stir up your spirit to be sensitive to the Spirit of God. When you pray in tongues, you open your spirit to the revelations of the Spirit of God. (1 Corinthians 2:10). Amos

3:7 says, *"Surely the Lord GOD does nothing Unless He reveals His secret to His servants the prophets."*
As you use your gift and speak more in tongues, your Spirit man is sensitive to pick up what the Lord is saying and doing.

- **Prophesy.** In the place of prayer, tell God your desire to prophesy. As you pray, open yourself up to the Holy Spirit. Remember, when you ask in faith, you receive. (Mark 11:24). Bind up any hindering spirit in Yasha (Jesus) Mighty Name. Now after you pray, quiet yourself and listen in your spirit to what the Spirit of God gives you. He may give you a word, a knowing, or a line. You may see in your spirit. He may show you a picture or it may even be like a video or a cartoon-like vision. Start with that. Say what you see. Say the words he gives you. Begin speaking. As you begin speaking, the Holy Spirit will give you the rest of the prophecy. Do not be scared to speak out. Speak boldly. Go ahead and prophesy. Be bold. Speak what the Spirit of God is giving you. Even if you feel afraid to say what the Spirit of God is giving you, don't block the flow of prophecy because of fear. Most times you won't get the prophecy all at once. So, just say what the Holy Spirit gives you. Prophesy can also be ignited in dreams...God prophetically speaks to us in dreams, to give a word or a warning for yourself or someone else. Keep a journal...pray, and wait for the interpretation of the dream then start with what the Lord gives you. As you step out in faith, He will surely give you the rest.

- **Keep Record.** Do keep a record of what the Lord is saying to you in prophecy. You may do so in a journal either online or in hardcopy. Having activated the Prophetic in you, The Holy Spirit can give a word to come at any time and you don't want to miss what God is saying. Then wait to release the word if ever. Sometimes he will speak or show you something only for you to go into your prayer closet and pray what he gives you without saying a word about what he shows you. However, if the Lord puts it in your heart to prophesy to someone right away, do so, for it will bless them. **The Purpose of Prophecy,** Paul said, *"...he who prophesies speaks edification and exhortation and comfort to men."* (1 Corinthians 14:3). The purpose of the flow of the Prophetic in you is to bless others. The manifestation is to edify the body of Christ.

This is the beginning of igniting the prophet in you. Boy, I tell you once the ignition of the fire of the holy spirit is lit within you, the supernatural lights up the prophetic in ways you can't imagine like hearing, seeing, smelling, feeling, tasting, and so much more. For those of you who walk into the office of the Prophet, this brings on a new meaning of ignition. The father's heart and mind come to the forefront of almost everything you do supernaturally. It just expede the office you walk in. The success of your call depends on igniting the prophetic in you!

Beloved, Now, I want you to stir up the gift of God in you. Activate the Ignition of the Prophetic in you. Build upon Speaking in tongues. Although you don't need to speak in tongues to operate in the prophetic. Tongues are a doorway to strengthening you supernaturally. As you walk the prophetic ministry through, you will find yourself flowing in the prophetic like never before. But don't stay at the doorway, flow into the Prophetic by going through the door. For this is the will of God for you.

Conclusion

Well, my beloved friends, I want to conclude this book by sharing this exhortation. The prophets declare the counsel of God, Which causes things to happen and bring favor to God's people. Prophets will bring it right from the spirit realm into the physical. God has consistently used prophets from the beginning and still today.

For Example…God, through the prophetic ministry of Agabus Acts 11:28, prepared the church for a coming famine. He also, used the prophetic ministry of Agabus, to prepare Paul for the persecution that was ahead of him in Jerusalem Acts 21:10-11. You must understand some still to this day do not reckon with prophets even though the Bible says, "Believe in the LORD your God, so shall ye be established; believe his prophets, so shall ye prosper." (2 Chron 20:20). Nevertheless, God is sending revelation through the same agency he has always been using, his prophets. In 1 Cor 14:3-5, Paul wrote to the church in Corinth, ***"But he who prophesies speaks edification and exhortation and comfort to men. He who speaks in a tongue edifies himself, but he who prophesies edifies the church. I wish you all spoke with tongues, but even more that you prophesied; for he who prophesies is greater than he who speaks with tongues, unless indeed he interprets, that the church may receive edification."*** Here, you can feel what Paul is trying to convey. It is God's heartbeat that every believer flows in the prophetic. Today, more than ever, it is imperative to flow in the prophetic.

It is important so that you can walk into God's plan for your life. ***"But as it is written: Eye has not seen, nor ear heard, Nor have entered into the heart of man The things which God has prepared for those who love Him But God has revealed them to us through His Spirit. For the Spirit searches all things, yes, the deep things of God"*** **(1 Cor 2:9-10).** This is with the prophetic and the gift of the prophet. It is the Spirit of God that reveals to you the things that God has planned for you in the prophetic. It is not found in anyone or anywhere but in God. The plans of God for your life are accessed through the bible and with the relationship of the Holy Spirit. He searches the deep things of God to reveal them to you. 1 Cor 2:12 confirms that. Beloved, I encourage you to allow the flow of the prophetic in your life through the holy spirit. Remember, every believer can flow in the prophetic. Romans 8:14 says ***"For as many as are led by the Spirit of God, these are sons of God."***

Since this is God's heartbeat for you as a believer, I have sought to, by the help of the Holy Spirit, in these few pages help you to understand the inception and operation of prophets in the lives of God's people over the years. I believe that you now know and understand the relevance of the prophetic ministry in the body of Christ and in your life today.

Never forget that you are to live a prophetic life even if you don't have the formal calling of a prophet. Stay sensitive to the movements of the Spirit and you will find yourself flowing in the rivers of prophecy. I desire that this book has not only blessed you but inspired you to flow in the prophetic. Be blessed!

Bibliography:

Willmington, Harold L. Old Testament Survey,
Willmington's Complete Guide to Bible Knowledge.
Wheaton Illinois: Tyndale House Publishers, Inc, 1992
Print.

Wood, Leon. The Prophets of Israel. Grand Rapids MI:
Baker Books, 1979. Print

Geisler, Norman L. A Popular Survey of the Old
Testament, Grand Rapids MI: Baker Book House
Company, 1977. Print.

Strong, James. The New Strong's Exhaustive
Concordance of the Bible. Nashville Tennessee: Thomas
Nelson, n.d. Print.

Russell, Rusty. "Bible history online maps, images,
articles, and resources for biblical history."
biblehistory.com

Notes

Notes

Notes

Notes